©2016 ILUMINA PRODUCCIONES, S.A. De C.V.
All rights reserved.

ISBN: 978-1-943488-01-8

No part of this publication may be reproduced, distributed, or transmitted in any form or by any means, including photocopying, recording, or other electronic or mechanical methods, without the prior written permission of the copyright holder. The infringement of such rights may constitute an offense against intellectual property.

Published by: Editorial ILUMINA S.A. de C.V.

Printed in Mexico
By Offset Santiago S.A. de C.V.
Río San Joaquín 436, Col. Ampliación Granada
CP 11520, México D.F.

Messy Mo in: It's good to be true!
First edition: June 2016

Layout and editorial design: Paola Alonso.
Conceptual Art: Rosa Maria Campos Cruz.
Editorial review: Shaula Vega. Jonathan Venguer.
Hector Fernandez.

Messy Mo in:
THE BIG TRUTH

Text and illustrations by BIBIANA DOMIT

Hi! My name is Mo.
My friends call me Messy Mo.
I'm not very tidy, but
I'm a lot of fun to be around!
I like playing video games, eating candy,
and laughing out loud.

I don't really like school.
But, one day I learned something
really cool.
Something I'll remember
for the rest of my life!

It was Monday morning and I was late for school as usual. In the classroom, everyone sat very quietly. At first, I thought they were sleeping, but then I remembered...

We had a math test that day!

I closed my eyes and remembered
the last time I went home with an F.
Oh no! I didn't want to make my mother sad again!

I tried to solve the math problems one by one.
But it was useless. Nothing! Nada!

I didn't understand a single one.
Exhausted, I lay my head on the desk.

Suddenly, I had a great idea!
I remembered a TV show where a boy who wasn't very good in school, switched his exam for that of the best student in the class.

What a fantastic idea, I thought.
"Now I just need to switch my test with Carlito's, and write my name over his."

I waited until everyone was done and offered to help Miss Lily carry the exams to her car.

On the way there I dropped the exams
When she wasn't looking I took Carlito's exam,
erased his name and wrote mine: MO.

That afternoon I went home thinking I had done the right thing. I sat on the couch, ate some tasty snacks and felt very relaxed.

The next morning I was late to school again, but this time, Miss Lily had a big smile on her face!

Out on the playground I felt very proud. Suddenly something in my stomach didn't feel quite right. Ouch! It really hurt!

I thought it was something I ate the day before. Maybe all those doughnuts.

I also thought that the uncomfortable feeling would soon go away.
But it stayed with me for one,
two and even three days!

By Friday I still felt very sick
In the classroom Miss Lily named me
"Leader of the Month"
I felt surprisingly ashamed.

She took the Big Star off Carlito's name
and placed it over mine.

I had always dreamt of having the Big Star,
but for some strange reason,
now that I had it, I felt even worse!

Feeling nauseous,
I closed my eyes trying to
understand what was making me
feel so bad?!

Suddenly, someone accidentally bumped into me.
It was Carlitos
"I'm sorry" he said shyly.

And just then, at that moment, I understood it all.
"Wait! I am the one who is sorry" I said.
"Now I know what is making me feel so sick."

I ran back to the classroom and told the truth in front of all my classmates.

When I got home, I also told my mom.

The next morning at school
I gave Carlitos the Big Star.

It was not easy, but telling
the truth made me
feel really good!

That day I learned that lying
is not a good choice.

Now I always tell the TRUTH
and I felt very good!

TULLYS

Messy Mo

This guy is trouble but fun! He loves junk food, video games and his electric guitar.
Mo has a little spider living in his hair. He is a complete mess and does poorly in school but he is a true friend. There is something about him that makes him extraordinary.

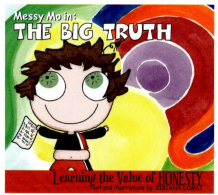

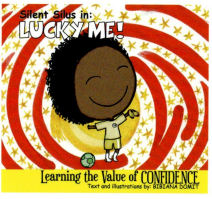
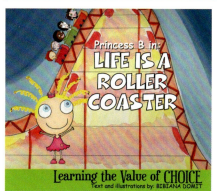
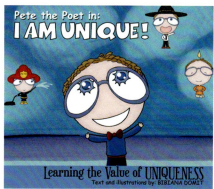
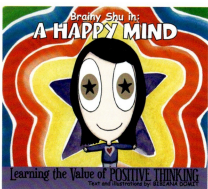

www.tullys.tv